Flotsam, Jetsam, L(

Collected Poems (in no particular order) from my coastal and local themed poetry pamphlets comprising of;

North Shields 'A Town Where No Town Ought To Be' 12 Poems of Time & Tide

As Tyne Goes By: 12 More Poems From The North East Coast

Drift Seed: 14 Poems of Root & Tide

Dean Jolly

Published By
All Write Up North Publishing

Dedicated To The North East Coast

My Very First Love

.

Thus o'er my pipe in contemplation
Of such things - I can constantly
Indulge in fruitful meditation,
And so, puffing contentedly,
On land, at sea, at home, abroad,
I smoke my pipe and worship God.

Excerpt from the poem Eddifying Thoughts of a
Tobacco Smoker by Johann Sebastian Bach

"We take a handful of sand from the endless
landscape of awareness around us and call that
handful of sand the world."

Excerpt from Zen and the Art of Motorcycle
Maintenance: An Inquiry Into Values by Robert M Pirsig

CONTENTS PAGE

Introduction

Welcome dear readers to the world of "Flotsam, Jetsam, Lagan, and Derelict" - a collection of coastal and local-themed poetry that takes you on a poetic journey along the North East coast. I am delighted to present to you this compilation of my poetic works, collected from my previous poetry pamphlets: *North Shields 'A Town Where No Town Ought To Be,' 12 Poems of Time & Tide, As Tyne Goes By*, and *Drift Seed.*

The inspiration behind this collection stems from my deep-rooted love for the North East coast, which I consider my first and most enduring love.

In these pages you will find a diverse array of poems that capture the essence of coastal living, the ebb and flow of time and tide, and the profound connections between humanity and the sea and each other. Each poem is a glimpse into moments of contemplation, memories held dear, and musings on life's journey.

You are invited to join me as I contemplate the vastness of the ocean, the legacy of those who came before and the ephemeral nature of our existence. Here, the power of the sea and the timeless rhythm of the tides serve as a backdrop for profound reflections on life's journey and the impermanence of it all. These verses also explore the fragments of our souls scattered across the shores, the sea as a symbol of loneliness and connection, and the delicate beauty of memories etched in the sands of time.

I hope you enjoy.

- Dean Jolly -

Turning The Tide

Troubles ebb and flow much like turning tide

Undulating waves of feast and famine

Remember this and take life in your stride

Never swim downstream be like the salmon

Insist on rising higher like a wave

Net your opportunities don't waste them

Gather every stone it's your path to pave

Tighten up your sails but never hasten

Hold your head as high as a damn mountain

Embrace the day ahead with but a smile

Turn troubled waters into spring or fountain

Insist that you must go the extra mile

Do these things and the tide may turn for you

Everybody else will benefit too

Time & Tide

I have learnt to treat Time and Tide as
One and the same
You see memories are like stones
Plucked from the beach
Older memories are half submerged by
The tide
Those ones are the smooth ones you
Find whilst looking for other things along
The shoreline and decide to keep and
Carry around for a while
The tide wears down the stone
Time wears down the memory
Until it is smooth enough to skip   across   a   Lake
Bad memories start off jagged and
Maybe time smoothes them or maybe
They stay jagged
Bad memories either sink or skip
Good memories are like sea glass
They are the shiny ones you find and take home
To make homemade jewellery
Bracelets made of different shades of
green and blue
and necklaces that shine when you hold
them up to the sun
so that you can wear your happiness around
your neck and feel good for a moment
Time and Tide smooth the stones
You can either sink them, skip them or
Turn them into jewellery

Notes On Coastal Living

I have made my peace with sunsets
And with tides that chart the Time
I have envied from a distance
Those large boats upon the Tyne
I have walked this mighty coastal stretch
From Shields as far as Amble
I have drank the Northern Waters
Ate blackberries from the bramble
I have touched the wooden dolly
with her host of hidden mice
I have written of her in my book
And now I do it twice
I have seen memorial benches
Above Fish Quay like holy pews
For those that knew a pretty sight
Of a peaceful river view
I have lived beside the coastline
All my life and it's still giving
I have learnt a lesson from its flow
Life goes on and life's for living!

An Old Sailors Reminisce

The river brought him home
To North Shields
Hyem sweet Hyem
Last port for an old sea dog
a retired Fisherman
Looking to rest
To reminisce
Oh there was nothing wrong
with his memory
nothing at all
Memories are just like
The fish in the sea
He would say
Easy to catch and harder to hold onto
But he held on all the same
He could still recall for instance
As a young lad
no more than seven or eight
The time he'd fallen into the Tyne
fished out by trawler men
His first real taste of the sea
Or a few years later
When he had found
A message in a bottle
washed up on King Edwards Bay
that simply read;
'If you find me, throw me back in the sea'
and nothing more
Back then it had made him chuckle
But now he didn't quite know
what to make of it
you see he couldn't bring himself to do it
so he had kept the bottle with him
Took it all over the world
Until it came to rest

on his mantle piece
And he didn't know why
He didn't just throw that damn bottle
Back to where it wanted to be
Just maybe he would take a walk
He thought to himself
down next to St Mary's Lighthouse
and throw it away
but in truth he was scared to
it had become
almost like a piece of his own soul
But then he thought
about the Old Wooden Doll
And just how many pieces
of that Doll
were scattered
across the shores
Little pieces of home
Spread to the four winds
Or else carried around in the pockets
of superstitious sailors...
Tomorrow!
He thought to himself
He'd do it tomorrow.
Next morning
Whilst it was still dark
He took the early bus into Tynemouth
and with bottle in hand
took the steep road
alongside Priory Castle down to
Priors Haven
In time for the sunrise
And after years of holding on
He let it all go
All at once
The tears
The bottle
The memories

All of it
When it was done he thought
Maybe he'll take a walk to Collingwood monument
Climb the steps
and go fishing for another memory
There was one
A memory that stood out
more so than the others
of a time when he had climbed those same steps
with a lover
and shared a kiss
as the sun went down over the bay
he remembered thinking...
Do you think God ever flicked paint at a canvas
to see what it would make?
If he did
don't you think
that he would have already known
where each fleck was going to fall?
What colours would find each other?
and that he was already going to call it a sunset?

As Tyne Goes By

He walked the coastline he walked as a young boy
With a mouth full of bitter seawater memories
Bare foot on the sands that could just as easily
Have been strewn from a cracked hourglass
The coast was awash with life
Dog walkers
Swimmers
Surfers
Old couples counting down sunsets
Children running from the ever changing tide
Dreamers
Joggers
Poets
Artists painting sunrises
Capturing the gold face of a new day
People gather here for something
Be it beauty or meaning or perhaps
They see in the vastness of the sea
A loneliness that rolls over them like a wave
He lit a cigarette and pondered on it
What does it mean to know that the sea will not
remember you?
What does it mean to know that the sun still sets over
the bay?
'Time and Tide'
He thought about those who walked this coastline
before him
Those who felt the same sting of cold northern winds
and of those who watched as the ocean carried boats
over the horizon
Gone now
out of sight
And he thought about his own life
A series of sunrises and sunsets
And of the hourglass spilling out the grains of new days

You see Time is a beach played on by innocent children
Wholly ignorant of the deadly current or staggering
depths of life
'Time and Tide'
His Mam and Dad used to say it
They were gone now too
The tide had long since swallowed them up
And all that remained were their ashes in two urns sat
on his mantelpiece.
He looked down to find water brushing at his feet
The tide was coming in
It was coming for him
'Not yet' he thought to himself
As he took a step back
It was then that he noticed it
A message in a bottle
A little out of reach but...
He stretched out and let the bottle float right into his
hand
Back home he set the bottle down on his living room
table and lit a cigarette
He let his imagination run wild as to what the message
might say
Finally after two more cigarettes he opened it up
No name
No address or telephone number
Nothing to identify the original messenger
It simply read
'If you find me, throw me back in the sea'
and nothing more.
And he thought about what it all meant
Sat for hours just looking at that bottle
Reading and then re-reading the note
Until he was down to his last cigarette
It occurred to him then that the bottle had
Probably been found many times
Touched Many lives and seen many shores
He knew then what was to be done

He took out a measure of his parents ashes and
siphoned them into the bottle
Then pen in hand he made an amendment to the
original note
The next day he drove to St Mary's Lighthouse and
tossed the bottle back into the sea
He could just about make out the rolled up note as the
bottle floated away
He smiled thinking about it
The new note read
'If you find us, throw us back in the sea'

My Favourite View Of All Is You

I've seen the sunset from the northern pier
I've seen a sky of red and gold stood here
Then later still silk stars over Tynemouth
And full grown moon glowing bright to the south
I've seen ferry's cut the Tyne in two
But my favourite view of all is you
I've seen the sunrise from King Edwards Bay
I've seen the orange flames of a new day
I've seen small pieces of sun in the sea
Like mirrored mosaic tiles they be
I've seen waters of the most deepest blue
But my favourite view of all is you
I've seen stones skipped at Priors Haven
I've seen a ship take her voyage maiden
I've seen St Mary's light her silent beacon
I've seen the oil black tide waters deepen
I've seen things I'd never think were true
But my favourite view of all is you

The Ferryweavers

Liken the Tyne

To the warp threads

On a loom

And the Ferryweavers

In their shuttle boats

Of Spirit and Pride

The weft that threads

And binds

North to South

South to North

A Tapestry

Of history

A Picture

Worth a thousand words

Under Howard Street

I often thought as one does wonder

Lost In musings when one walks to work

What hides neath Howard Street I'd ponder

And in indulgence of my harmless quirk;

A Gas Main? Certainly! But was there more?

A Treasure Chest? No! Surely closer to the shore?

A smokers pipe? Perhaps once bought from local store?

A secret room? But where then would you find the door?

Then workmen came armed with their blackened spades

and drills and cones and bricks and metal signs

They found no smokers pipe nor secret place

For the treasure chest was old tram lines!

Friends Of The Quay

An evening's lark along the fish quay

with work weary friends we seekers of glee

Quick nip to the dog of the salty sea

then to the Low Lights for a pint or three

Where music carries like an ocean spray

from guitars and mouths; Such great revelry

One more for the road the lads they did say

Yet last orders bell was still quite a way

So Chris got the round and Tom rolled a smoke

And I told Aaron a god awful joke

Damon listened as guitar strings were stroked

We stayed there all night until we were broke.

I Met A Man From Ukraine

I met a man from Ukraine

On lower Howard Street

Where the Stag Line anchor

sits against a back drop of the Tyne

He was watching the ferry cross

From North Shields To South Shields

He smiled when he saw us

We were sat on a nearby bench

My partner and I

And a 4 year old and 5 day old newborn baby

He wished us well and told us of the horrors back at home

His son was a soldier

His wife was in the dole office

He could not work out

Why man inflicts pain on man

Or why the simple beauty

Of a river view

Was not enough

For some people

A Tribute To Tommy Brown
Encoded In Enigma

ispof xjqpi phcls ibeta gvcks bcqri cwdvv ihzhg rmarq qrxjw iraly
rjvgo ydozo ldogq nyubu adbze epwek qknaj ihpuk emjin psppq iufwl
nueel fwmiw lgisz hhmyr aernj zvtmh waiob

Directions For Decryption

Visit Cryptii.com

Choose Following Enigma Model: *Enigma 1*
Set Reflector: UKWB
Set Rotor 1: l position: 20T Ring: 15O
Rotor 2: l Position: 13M Ring: 13M Rotor 3: lll Position:
25Y Ring: 2B

*Note the letters in the sequence spell out TOMMYB

Princess Seaways

She took her seat
Alongside the other day-trippers
And watched as the last stragglers
Boarded the busy coach back to the boat
In the roots of Amsterdam she had blossomed
Dropped
Smiles
Like
They
Were
Petals
In
The
Wind
One floated
Down
From a bridge she's only ever seen
In postcards
And found its way
Onto the face of a young child
She'd took pictures
Figured she's use them for a scrapbook
And yet what is a picture? But a window
On a boat going home
The coach doors closed
Her eyes closed
and when they opened again
The boat was waiting
Back onboard
she wandered
the narrow corridors
of her mind
her thoughts turned to home
to North Shields
'A town where no town ought to be'

She had read that on a sign
It's ok she thought to live in a town
Where no town ought to be
If beauty can thrive along its shores
The thought made her
Drop
Another
Petal
And she retired to her room to sleep
She dreamt of the sea and of a great ribbon
That wrapped itself around her
It was pulling her towards
The future
In the morning she woke early
Grabbed her bags and her camera
And made her way to the skybar
She wanted one more photograph
A picture of her hometown
From the sea
And as she took it
The landscaped grinned from pier to pier
Dropping
It's
Own
petals

The Taxi Driver

The taxi driver spoke at length
Of a chalet back in Spain
Time spent with his wife abroad
And of the many friends they met
And lost to time and ill health
He had taken up taxiing after his wife had passed away
She listened as a Doctor would listen
Diagnosing him in need of another holiday
Yet wondering if he'd ever make it back to that same chalet
She hoped some day that he would
And that maybe the walls would still hold
The kind of laughter that sticks
And that there he could be with his wife once again
She asked if she could take his picture
He was more than happy to oblige
The scrapbooks had grown larger
The pictures sometimes dog eared around the edges
Faded windows
She would keep the picture of the taxi driver for many years
Taking it out every now and again
Thinking of that chalet and what it meant
To have memories of a place she never even visited
Or what it meant to catch a glimpse of other people's lives
All travelling and yet all standing still
She never saw him again
And so never did find out
If he ever made it home

Tynemouth Market

A Tyne Bridge coaster
An old vaudeville poster
A print of the priory
A cane made of wood and ivory
Sea glass from Longsands
Sculpted driftwood by artists hand
Broken keys and locks
A photograph of smith's docks
Roses made from metal
A rusty tin kettle
Plants of every shape and manner
Chisels, hammers and even a spanner
Collectibles of every taste
From world war one to wall hung plates
Murano clowns and books abound
On every topic you could expound
Homemade candles
Antique door handles
Cherry blossom coloured sandals
Vintage dinky and matchbox cars
Pub signage from the old seven stars
All these treasures could be yours if you want it
When you take a day trip to Tynemouth Market

Three Haiku's

The seagulls take flight

Yearning for Northern Waters

Nothing but blue hues

Enchanted Coastline

Muse of Poets and Playwrights

Ode to Oceanus

Untold history

Tynemouth reveals old secrets

Her mouth wide open

Our Harvest Is From The Deep

Our harvest was not borne in the fields
but from the deep
They were earthy yields
From neath our feet

Our harvest was not veg nor corn
but fish and coal
caesarean born
Blackened earth and swimming shoal

Our harvest was no farmers chore
but the Miners and the Fishermens mission
Who dug the land and trawled the shore
Enduring despite harsh condition

Let our harvest and our history be revealed
Like the land itself upon which we used to reap
For our heritage still lives on in old North Shields
So behold our harvest from the deep

Your Little Boat Went Out Of Sight

Your little boat went out of sight

I watched it fade into the night

And of its burning lantern lights

Once glowing yet no longer bright

Your little boat beyond my eye

'Pon sea of salty tears I cried

From shore to where the sea meets sky

I watched your little boat sail by

Your little boat no longer near

Cast out and gone beyond the pier

But though you are no longer here

Your memories remain my dear

Murmuration

I saw them once those early sun rise birds

Starlings in murmuration I did glance

And yet back then I did not know that word

I only marvelled at their starling dance

Beauty came before the definition

Like when we met I didn't know your name

But knew somehow through blind recognition

By meeting you life wouldn't be the same

Birds and hearts both fly in murmuration

Both you and I in starling dance as one

We sent our troubles south in migration

And what remained was love when they were gone

Bard From The Pub

Beer drunk poet sat in a beer garden

Alone with his thoughts his glass half empty

Rolling a cigarette as sky darkens

Down to his last four pound and a twenty

Famish and thirst; Frightful drinking partners

Rich is the man who needs nothing at all

Only a poet, a drunk and Sartre

Make you question the writing on the wall

Truth is not in the bottom of a glass

Hope is not in the pump nor the pint

Envy is a bitter served from the brass

Peace is a glow of a match in the night

Until the sound of the last orders bell

Beer drunk poet sits pondering for a spell

A Remember When A Was A Bairn

A remember when a was a bairn
Gannin' to Whitehouse Primary School
Mornin' assemblies with Mr Maxwell
and Mrs Lewis and Mrs Watson as well

A remember when a was a bairn
Comin' home from school to hyem
Was anly through the cut
Whey it was less than ten minutes on foot

A remember when a was a bairn
Six weeks holidays in the summer
Outside with me best mate
If the street lights turned on you were late

A remember when a was a bairn
If ye were told ye wa gannin
Alang the road to Whitley bay
Well it was like a holiday

A remember when a was a bairn
me mam gannin doon North Shields
alang unicorn house we went
to pay the monthly rent

A remember when a was a bairn
gannin to me nana's hoose
From Barnstaple to Lynn Road
For a cup of tea and a slice of toast

A remember when a was a bairn
The chocolate eggs looked bigger
And we painted real eggs for competition
Cle-eggpatra, Sonic the eggchog a real egg-hibition

A remember when a was a bairn
Dressing up for Halloween
Me costume was a black bin liner
And the sweets well ye couldn't get finer

A remember when a was a bairn
A was in the Christmas nativity
A played a shepherd with cut out sheep
And the kings had crowns made out of crepe

A remember when a was a bairn
On Sundays you wore your best
Went to your nanas for sunday roast
Or took a trip in the car alang the coast

Aye, a remember when a was a bairn
If love was money I'd have been a millionaire
Even though we had nowt
We never did go without.

Drift Seed

Sea beans carried without clear direction

Upon the whims of the northern waters

Deep rooted by a coastal connection

Drift seeds scattered to the four quarters

Like messages in bottles boldly cast

Penned by lovers; a romantic notion

Or the sailor fixing sails to his mast

To set out far and explore the ocean

There's a such same aimlessness in drift wood

And jetsam that overboard is tossed

Each one adrift drift seed upon the flood

But not all those that float are truly lost.

We Are As DriftWood

We are as driftwood

Whittled into splendour

Washed up by the sea

Plucked from the shore

And placed into the pocket

Of one who sees the beauty

In what was once lost.

The Empty Wood

Is there a solitude
In the deep roots
Of old trees
Within the denseness
Of an empty wood?

Is there a loneliness
In the shallow waters
Of a forgotten stream
Without a witness
To its gentle flow
Within the denseness
Of the empty wood?

Are there forgotten dreams
In the deep heart
Of a wishing well
That touch the same roots
And the same stream
Of the empty wood?

Memories of A Childhood By The Sea

Memories of a childhood by the sea

He wears like a string of assorted pearls

Tahitian, Akoya, Baroque, Keshi

Made from Nacre like a Nautilus Whorl

Time has stripped them of their moonlight luster

But the tide brings back their shimmering tint

And those pearls pulled from that bed of oysters

Retain a sleek and scintillating glint

Memories of a childhood by the sea

A torsade of waves made with silken strands

Spanning from Tynemouth to North Shields

For he grew up there on the northeast sands

Sonnet To The Sea

Siren songs of a lonely lament sings she

Of a time when her beauty was lauded

Northern compass Queen of the seven seas

Netting lovers through the ships she boarded

Ending lives by the cruel whim of her tides

The sea does not truly love only lusts

Then sends them off to their watery graves

Only the dead her true soul she entrusts

Trust not her ebb and flow she is not tame

Her nature hides behind a shallow veil

Empires comes and go yet she remains

Searching for a lover to change her ways

Ever changing yet constant is the sea

Although she will never remember thee

Shell I Tell You

Shell I tell you of the Baltic Tellin?

As common as the grey-white heron

Shell I tell you of the pointed Auger?

Long thin snail huts by the Water

Shell I tell you of the Periwinkle?

Found around the coastline sprinkled

Shell I tell you of the Banded Wedge Shell?

Bivalve Mollusc half sunk by the swell

Shell I tell you of the brown Blunt Gapers?

Found in lower mud sand substrata

Shell I tell the humble Limpets of thee?

As they cling to rocks in ubiquity

Yes I Shell.

Fathom

Fathom the Sea

Fathom the blues

Fathom the depth of darkened hues

Fathom the Moon

Fathom the greys

Fathom the shallow tide of days

Fathom the sand

Fathom the yellows

Fathom the sea and moon as strange bed fellows

Undercurrent

Tides are expected

Observable

Cyclical in nature

It is not the tide

But the unseen

Unobserved

Constant

Yet unpredictable

Undercurrent

That can sweep you away

Remember this above all else

Next time you step into my waters

The Talent Of The Unknown Busker

I stopped to watch a busker on the high street

Where the clock and the entrance to The Beacon meet

Strumming on a worn out acoustic guitar

A funked up rendition of Whiskey In The Jar

Whilst the throng of the Christmas shopping brigade

Didn't listen and simply carried on with their day

I gave him some change and he tipped me his hat

And I went on my way and that was that

Later that day I saw the man packing up

Counting a handful of change tipped from inside his cup

Five hours of busking his heart and his soul

For a couple of quid and a Greggs sausage roll

Between You, Me & The Stan Laurel Statue

I told you your troubles

As you told me mine

We promised each other

It would stay

Between you me and the Stan Laurel Statue

Old Stan scratched his head

Laughed as he listened

Watched as we kissed

Wondered why

Two souls needed

The ears of a statue

A comedian as a confidante

But then maybe a serious word

Needs a comedic ear

Or a serious ear

Needs a comedic word

A Town Where No Town Ought To Be

I was born here
In a town where no town ought to be
but here it sits
Here it endures
Defiant
Like the people of this place
Hardy
That's perhaps a more apt word for it
Stan Laurel was familiar with 'Hardy'
Before he ever met Oliver
Having been born here too
I'd like to think
That old Stan would have found that one funny
You see laughter is born in hardship
And times were hard
In a town where no town ought to be
Yet in the wake of the ships leaving
other ships took their place
Friendships
kinships
Companionships
Those ships stayed
They dropped
anchor
in
the
hearts
of
the
people
who
lived
In a town where no town ought to be

Terms of Endearment

He's a canny bloke
Vic from the pub
Always gets a round in
Never causes any trouble
Heart of gold really
Salt of the earth
Likes a drink
Likes to roll his own cigarettes
With a fifty gram pouch of turner
Menthol tips
Smoking
In North Shields town centre
You'd see him riding
On his bike
Down Tynemouth Road
Everyone knows the route
Passed King Street Club
Then a turn at Tynemouth Lodge
On to Tanners Bank
Ride passed the Low Lights
Get some fish and chips for his mam
He did it most days
Aye he's a canny bloke
Vic from the pub

View From A Car Window

There is a secret in the distant hills

There is a certain colour green that thrills

There is melancholy in empty fields

Through the car window as I leave North Shields

On a journey of many winding roads

A poet ponders Elegies and Odes

And everything that he has left aside

Is everything that's still frozen in time

The moment and the memory collides

Long after the setting sun falls behind

Huscrofts Clock

Huscrofts clock can't salvage time

But Huscrofts shop reclaims antique signs.

Huscrofts clock can't backwards tock

But Huscrofts shop sells salvaged stock

Huscrofts clock can't slow the years

But Huscrofts shop holds vintage wares

Huscrofts clock can't hold time fast

But Huscrofts shop contains the past

For My Friends At The Seven Stars

At the seven stars I buy my first pint
John's on his third Thistly Cross of the night
The beer garden's lovely this time of day
Last of the sun slowly moving away
Gajy appears with his signature hat
and smiles at us with his face full of tats
Out comes our pat with a vape and a drink
She says her John's let her out of the clink
Then out through the door comes Pickled Onion Steve
Whose nickname I still cannot quite believe
Even Ernie who plays the church organ
Isn't called organ Ernie but that's not important
I pop back inside and Rob pours me another
And low and behold there stands Dylan my Brother
Drinking a Guinness with Matt and Keaton
A right regular old mother's meeting!
Michael and lez stand there doing the crossword
Stuck on three across 'An Exotic Bird'
Lez thinks it's a Motmot but 3 down is showing Lupin
Which makes me suspect that it must be a Toucan
If you fancy a good old fashioned boozer
With interesting folk it ain't no snoozer
This one of a kind isn't like other bars
So aim for the good old Seven Stars

God Only Knows

I read somewhere
That there are more stars
Than there are grains of sand
On the earth
That's perspective!
Maybe we should stop
And think about that for a moment
When we go about our daily lives
Like how many atoms
Make up your Costa Coffee
Or how it takes eight minutes
For the light from the sun
To reach your eyes
So that you could look at a restaurant menu
Or how we are the universe
Experiencing itself
And perhaps you'll say
But what about God?
You see I also read somewhere
That as much as God Is all knowing
The one thing he couldn't know
Is what a universe would be like
Without him In it
So he made it so
And the big bang
Was God splitting himself
Into what is
And what has always been
And each living thing
Is God
Experiencing first hand
His creation

Love & Cigarettes (Revisited)

I met her in a pub in North Shields
Of course I did
I was standing in the doorway
Of the Bell & Bucket
Lighting
The most important cigarette of my life
As she passed me by
Yet life is a funny thing
You see I knew as I walked back in
That I would find her
Sitting on the next table over
from mine
well...
at first I said nothing
it wasn't that I couldn't
but what was I supposed to say?
Talk about the weather?
My love of rain?
As we drank
The bar played Fleetwood Mac
From a small tv screen
Bracketed to the wall
And out the corner of my eye
She took a drink and danced to herself

She knew the song

'I love Fleetwood mac too' I said

And we both agreed that we loved

The Chain and Dreams and Gypsy

She even smoked too

I still remember the warning on the front

Of my backy pouch as she rolled me a cigarette

It said 'smoking seriously harms you and others around you'

And I remember thinking

'no more thank drinking I suppose'

'no more than love'

Drinking

Smoking

Love

They all have their own addiction

But only two of them come with warning labels

But I didn't think

That love could pass me in a doorway

Or that I would find myself

Sharing a cigarette

With a woman I had only just met

Or dreamt about without knowing her name

Or that years would pass

And the colours in the embers of that cigarette

Could still burn as strong

Smoke & Sky

I saw the beauty in an evening cigarette

Stood at the top step

Half leaning against the back door

Observing a half crescent moon

A few scattered stars

And the yellow glow

From neighbouring windows

Printed in Great Britain
by Amazon

45617312R00030